How & Why
Animals Grow New Parts

Most starfish are shaped like five-pointed stars. But this starfish was attacked by a hungry fish. Three of its arms are gone! Will this be the end of the starfish?

Not at all. The missing arms begin to grow back. Before long, the starfish is whole again.

The starfish is one of a small group of animals with an amazing ability. These animals can grow new body parts.

A robin tries to pull an earthworm from the ground. But the bird gets only part of the worm. Will the worm die?

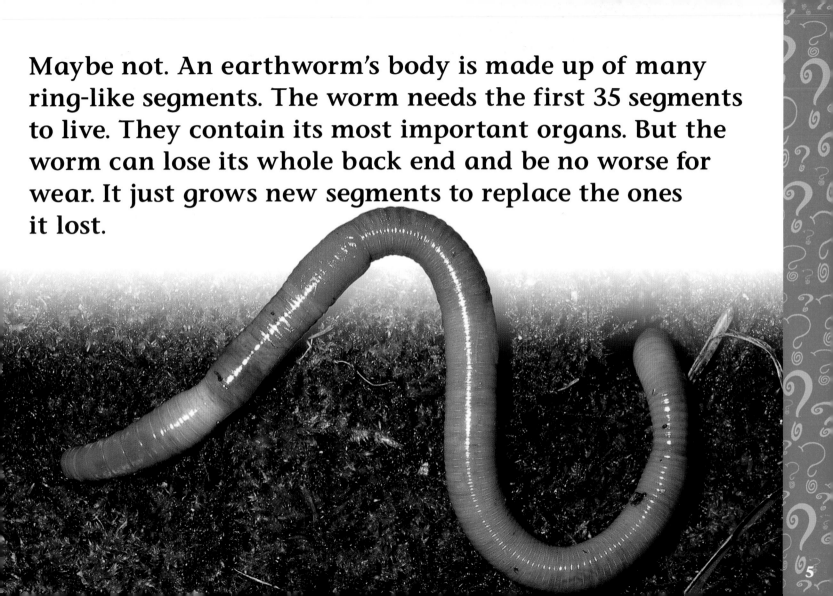

Maybe not. An earthworm's body is made up of many ring-like segments. The worm needs the first 35 segments to live. They contain its most important organs. But the worm can lose its whole back end and be no worse for wear. It just grows new segments to replace the ones it lost.

The planarian flatworm lives in water. It is small, but it is a champion at replacing body parts.

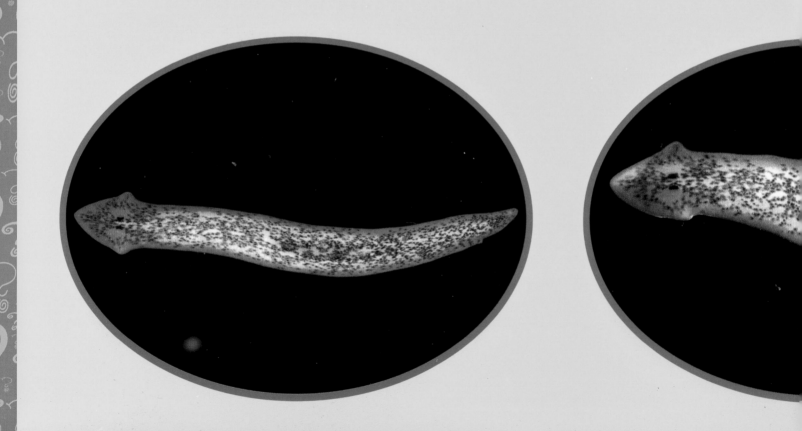

If the flatworm loses its tail, it grows a new one. And if it loses its head, it grows a new head! Most animals that grow new parts are simple, like worms. But some more complex animals can do this, too.

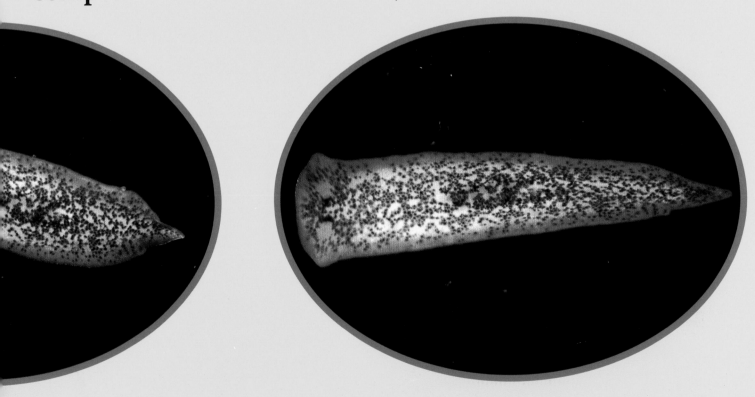

This anole *(uh-no-lee)* lizard would make a tasty meal for a bird or another hungry animal. But the lizard fools its enemies with a trick.

When the hunter tries to grab the lizard, the end of the lizard's tail breaks off! The tail lies wiggling on the ground, and the lizard runs away. Soon it grows a new tail.

A dragonfly nymph attacks a tadpole and bites its tail. But the tadpole struggles free and swims away, leaving its tail behind.

Soon its tail begins to grow back. The tadpole survives the attack because it can lose its tail and grow a new one.

This salamander has had a close call. Look carefully at its leg, just below its feathery gills. The toes and part of the leg are missing. Maybe they were bitten off by a fish. But the salamander escaped.

Before long, the missing leg and toes grow back. The salamander is as good as new.

Crayfish and crabs can grow new legs and claws. If a crayfish or crab loses a claw or one of its smaller walking legs, a new part begins to grow right away.

Growing new parts is one of many abilities that help these animals survive.

Use the information in this book to answer some "how and why" questions.

- How does a starfish get back lost arms?

- Why does the earthworm need its first 35 segments to live?

- Why is the planarian flatworm a champion at replacing body parts?

- How does the anole lizard fool its enemies?

- How does the tadpole survive an attack?

- How does growing new parts help crabs and crayfish?